My Eyes

Kathy Furgang

The Rosen Publishing Group's
PowerKids Press™
New York

For Linda

Published in 2001 by The Rosen Publishing Group, Inc.
29 East 21st Street, New York, NY 10010

First Edition

Book Design: Kim Sonsky

Illustration Credits: All organ 3-D illustrations © LifeArt/TechPool Studios, Inc.; All other 3-D illustrations by Kim Sonsky.

Furgang, Kathy.
   My eyes/ by Kathy Furgang.
      p. cm.—(My body)
   Includes Index.
   Summary: Explains the parts of our eyes, how they allow us to see in color and darkness, the importance of good vision, and various eye problems.
      ISBN 0-8239-5573-7 (alk. paper)
      1. Eye—Juvenile literature. 2. Vision—Juvenile literature. [1. Eye. 2. Vision. 3. Senses and sensation.] I. Title.

QP475.7 .F87 2000
   612.8'4—dc21   99-045245

Manufactured in the United States of America

Contents

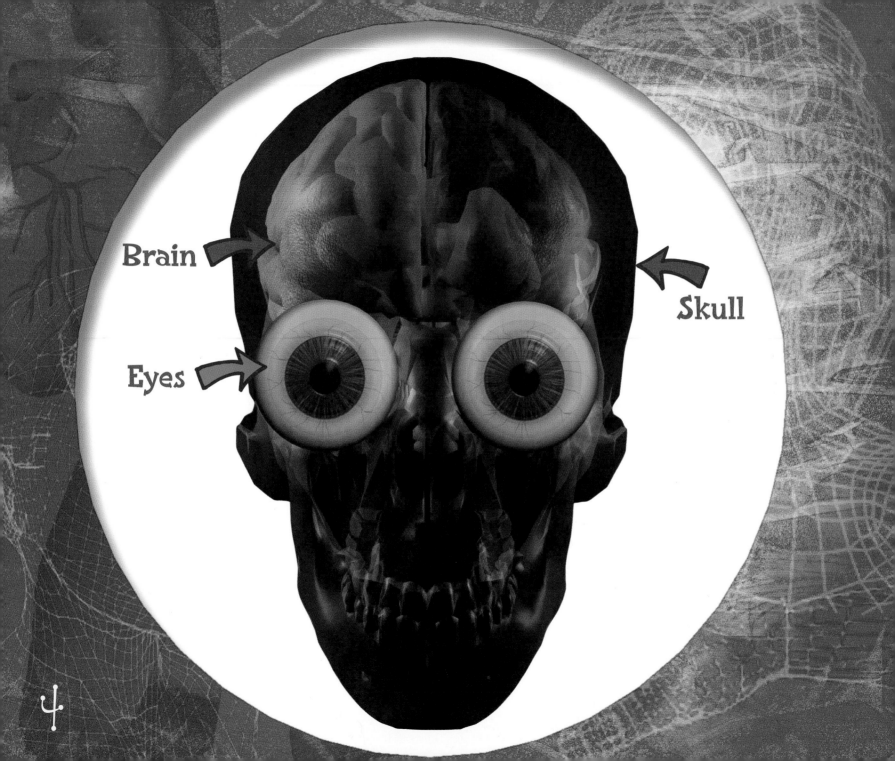

Amazing Eyes

If you can read these words or see the pictures on these pages, then your eyes and your brain are hard at work. Your eyes, ears, nose, and tongue are all sense organs. A sense organ is a body part that helps your brain understand things about the world that surrounds you. Your eyes work by taking in light from all around you. When the light travels to the inside of your eyes, messages are sent to your brain. Your brain uses these messages to tell you what you are seeing.

Sight is one of our five senses. The other senses are hearing, touch, taste, and smell.

A Good Pupil

Light enters your eyes through a clear, curved layer called the **cornea**. The cornea is thin and strong. Light then passes through the small black circle in each of your eyes. This small circle is called the **pupil**. Your pupils are always changing size. They become larger and smaller to let the right amount of light into your eyes. The colored part of your eye, the **iris**, surrounds the pupil. Your iris is a muscle that moves to make your pupils bigger or smaller. There is something in your iris called **melanin** that gives it color. Darker eyes have more melanin than lighter eyes.

When it is dark, your pupils become larger to let more light into your eyes. Blue eyes and light colored eyes are more sensitive to bright sunlight.

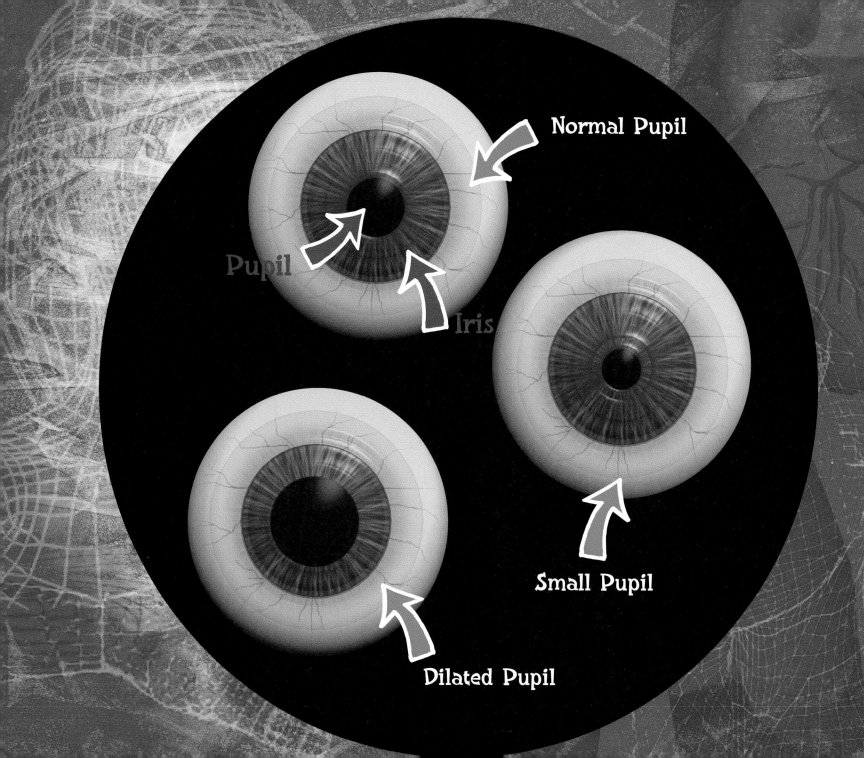

Normal Pupil

Pupil

Iris

Small Pupil

Dilated Pupil

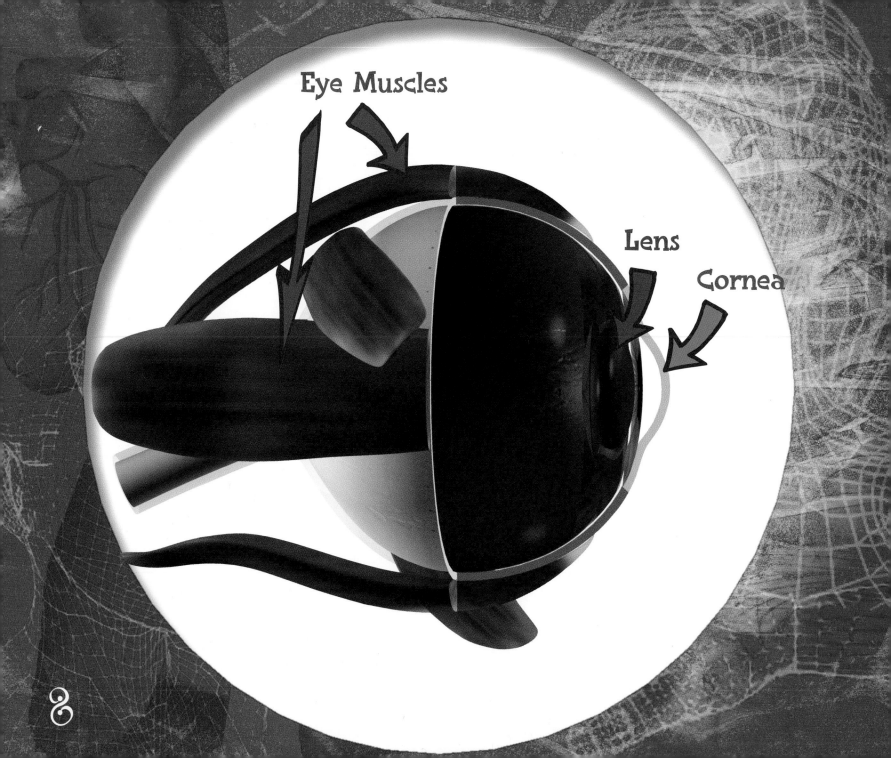

Eyes Like a Camera

Your eyes work like a camera to help you see. Both your eyes and a camera need light to work. Neither would be able to work without a **lens**. Each eye has a lens shaped like an oval. It is found near the front of your eye, behind the cornea, iris, and pupil. After light enters your pupil, it reaches your lens. Look up at something across the room. Then look back down at this page. The lenses in your eyes had to **focus** twice. That means they had to change shape to see both objects clearly. Camera lenses are curved, and so are the lenses in your eyes. Tiny muscles squeeze and pull your lenses to help you see clearly.

Focusing takes practice. Newborn babies cannot yet focus their eyes to see things clearly. They also have trouble moving their eyes to look at things around them.

The Retina

Since the lenses in your eyes are curved, they bend light and turn the image you see upside down! Your lenses focus the upside-down image onto a spot on the back of your eye called the **retina**. The retina is very **sensitive** to light. It is also covered with tiny **nerve cells**. The nerve cells turn the light into messages, which are then sent to the brain. These messages travel through the **optic nerve**. The optic nerve begins at the back of the eye and goes to your brain. Your brain then turns the image right side up and tells you what you are seeing.

The eyes' lenses turn this image of a frog upside down. The lenses focus the image on the retina, which is covered with nerve cells. Messages from the nerve cells travel to the brain. It is the brain that turns the image right side up.

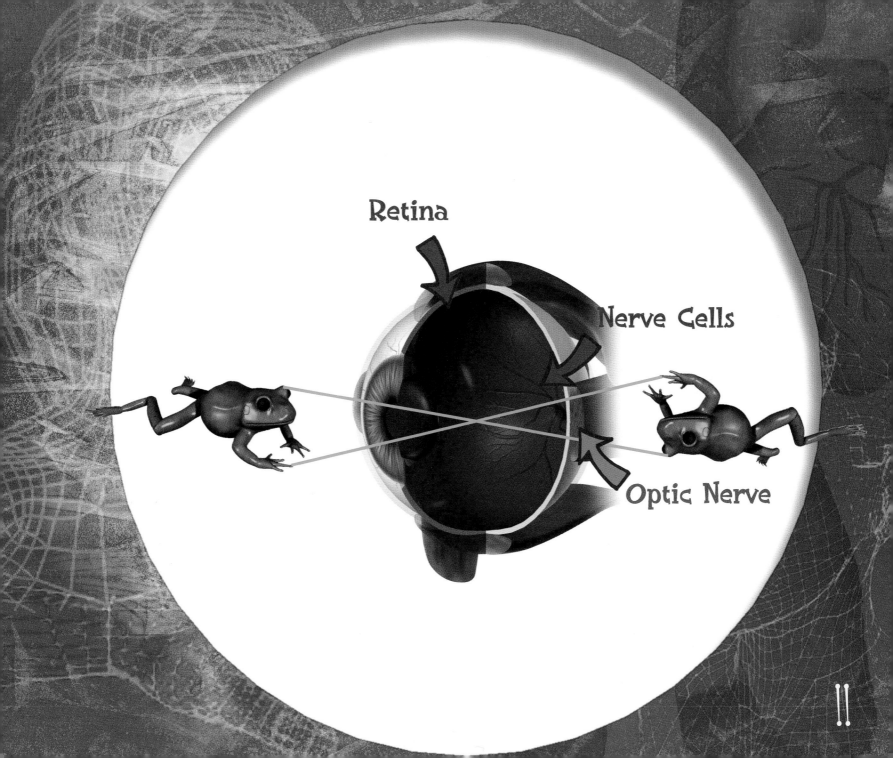

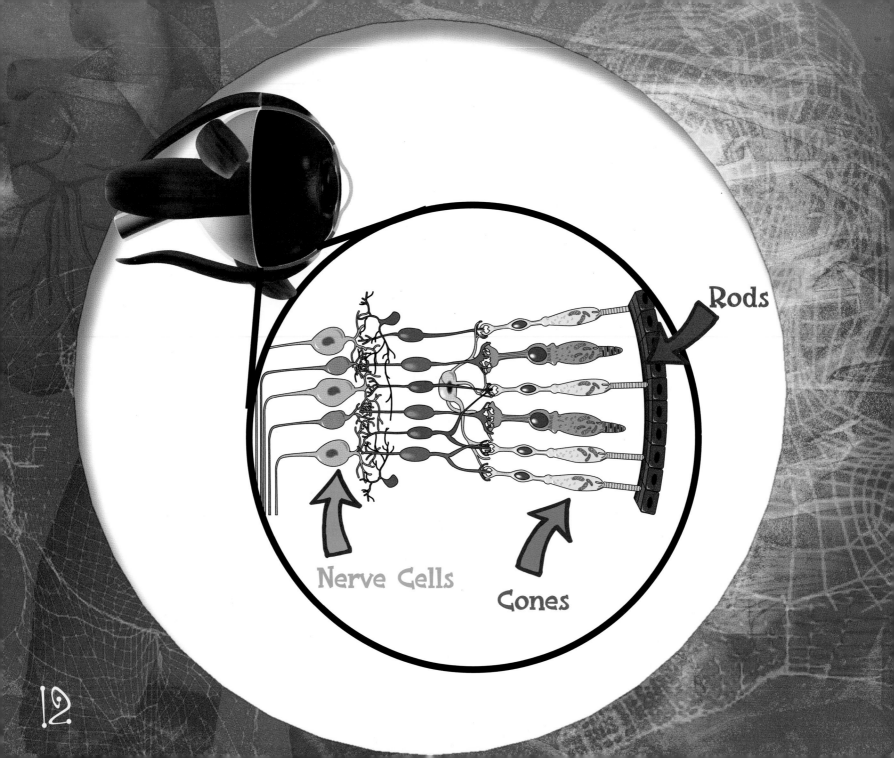

Seeing Color and Seeing in Darkness

How do your eyes see colors? Your retina is covered with tiny cells called **cones**. The human eye has seven million cones on each retina. The cones let you know what colors things are. People can tell the difference between up to 10 million shades of color! How do your eyes see outside at night? Your retina also has special cells called **rods** that let you see in very low light. Rods only allow you to see shades of gray. Most people have about 125 million rods on each retina.

People who cannot see the full range of colors are color-blind. The most common type is red-green color blindness. People who have this color blindness have trouble telling the difference between reds, greens, and browns.

13

Keeping Your Eyes Safe

Your eyes are protected in many ways. Your eyebrows and eyelashes help to keep sweat and dirt from getting into your eyes. You have a **tear gland** above each eyelid that keeps your eyes wet all the time. Tears have a chemical in them that kills germs. Tears are made in the tear gland. Then they move into the eye through a passageway called a **tear duct**. When you blink, your eyelids act like windshield wipers to wash tears and dust away. Your eyes fit inside two round holes in your skull. Your skull is shaped a certain way so that the hard bones around your eyes and nose help keep your eyes safe from harm.

You have a small tube called the lacrimal sac that connects each of your eyes to your nose. When you cry, your eyes make lots of tears. The tears go down this tube and then you have to blow your nose.

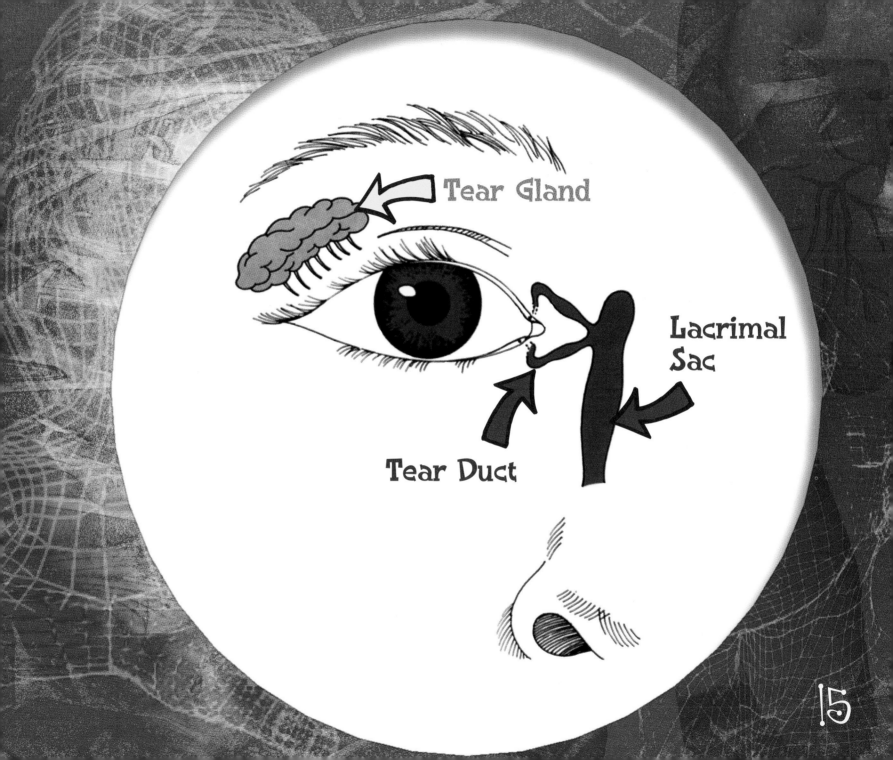

Tear Gland

Lacrimal Sac

Tear Duct

15

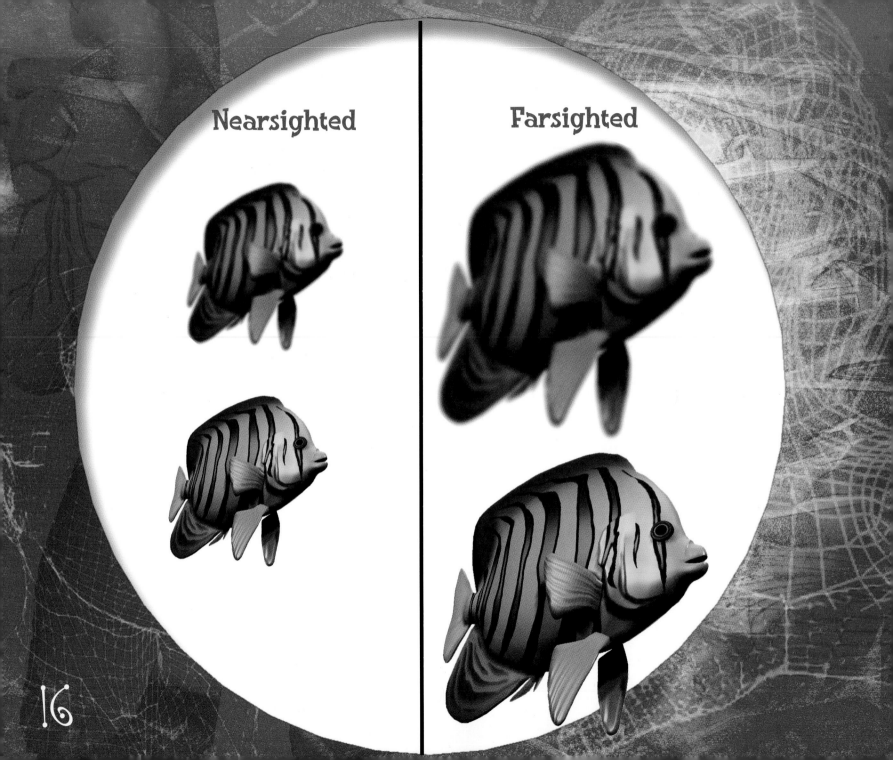

Nearsighted

Farsighted

16

A Visit to the Eye Doctor

Some people have better eyesight than others. When things that are far away from you look blurry, your eyes are nearsighted. This means that you can only see clearly the things that are close to you. When things that are close to you look blurry, your eyes are farsighted. This means that you can only see clearly the things that are far away. Nearsighted and farsighted people both have problems focusing light correctly on their retina. An eye doctor can give these people eyeglasses with lenses that are shaped to fix the problem.

People of all ages may need to wear glasses to see well. These pictures of fish show what things look like to nearsighted and farsighted people.

Two Eyes Are Better Than One

Why do you have two eyes? One good reason is that you can see more with two eyes than with just one. Your left eye can see things that are more to the left of you and your right eye can see things that are more to the right of you. Another reason two eyes are better than one is that having two eyes allows you to see how far away things are. Since your eyes are about two inches away from each other, each one sees the world from a different angle. When your brain puts the information from both of your eyes together, you see **depth**.

Each of your eyes has its own field of view. This means that each eye sees objects from different angles. The brain takes in the two views of the object, allowing us to see depth.

Right Field
of View

Left Field
of View

CATS IN THE AMERICAS

19

Eye Problems

One common problem that can happen to the eye is called pink eye. There is a clear, delicate layer that covers the front of the eye to protect it. When germs attack this layer, it can cause pink eye. This illness makes your eye red and itchy. Medicine can make pink eye go away. Sometimes people get a scratch on their cornea, the layer that keeps the eye safe. It hurts to have a scratched cornea, but with good care your eye can heal itself quickly. When people cannot see at all, it means that they are blind. Some people are born blind because parts of their eyes do not work properly. Other people become blind from accidents or certain illnesses.

When people have pink eye or a scratch on their cornea, they may have to wear a patch to protect the injured eye. Covering one eye can make the eye muscles weak. When the patch comes off, the eye will become strong again.

Seeing Without Sight

Imagine a world where you could not see at all. How would you read or safely cross the street? People who are blind have many ways of doing things without sight. They use a special alphabet, called Braille, to read. Braille is made of raised dots that can be felt by your fingers, instead of being seen by your eyes. Dog guides are dogs trained to help people who are blind. They help them cross the street, ride on trains, and get to stores. People who are blind also rely more on their other senses to learn about the world around them.

A   B   C   D   E

Glossary

cones (KONZ) Special cells in the back of the eyes that allow us to see colors.

cornea (KOR-nee-ah) The clear, strong outer layer of the eye that keeps it from harm.

depth (DEPTH) The distance of something from front to back.

focus (FOH-kis) To make clear.

iris (IY-ris) The round muscle in the eye that is colored and surrounds the pupil.

lens (LENZ) The clear, curved part of the eye that focuses light.

melanin (MEL-ah-nin) The substance that gives the iris its color.

nerve cells (NURV SELZ) Tiny fibers that carry information from the brain to places all around the body.

optic nerve (OP-tik NURV) The small tube that carries messages from the eye to the brain.

pupil (PEW-pul) The opening in the eye that changes size to let the right amount of light into the eye.

retina (RET-in-ah) The back wall of the eye that is very sensitive to light.

rods (RODZ) Nerve cells in the back of the eyes that allow us to see in dim lighting.

sensitive (SEN-sih-tiv) Being able to see small differences.

tear duct (TEER DUKT) The path between the tear gland and the eye.

tear gland (TEER GLAND) The part of your body that makes tears.

23

Index

Web Sites

To learn more about the eyes, check out this Web site:
www.brainpop.com/health/senses/vision/index.asp